Made in the USA
Las Vegas, NV
20 May 2023

72263374R00061